I0785467

Don't Make This $15,000 Self-Publishing Mistake

How to Effectively Count the Financial Cost of Becoming a Self-Published Author

Don't Make This $15,000 Self-Publishing Mistake

How to Effectively Count the Financial Cost of Becoming a Self-Published Author

JILL-CAPRI SIMMS

Edited by Dale Slongwhite, WriteLines.net

Liberating Truth

A division of Plumb Line Consulting, LLC

Don't Make This $15,000 Self-Publishing Mistake

How to Effectively Count the Financial Cost of Becoming a Self-Published Author

Copyright © 2018 by Jill-Capri Simms

ISBN-13: 978-1722435950
ISBN-10: 172243595X

Published by:
Liberating Truth
A division of Plumb Line Consulting, LLC
Windermere, FL
info@plumblineconsultinghr.com
www.plumblineconsultinghr.com

These are true stories. However, some names and places have been changed based on the author's discretion.
Printed in the United States.

DEDICATION

This book is dedicated to aspiring and published writers and authors whose passion is to get their literary work into the hands of readers in the most cost-efficient manner.

ACKNOWLEDGEMENTS

I thank Pastor Richard Meadows and Sister Linda Meadows, authors, editors and publishers who showed me the ropes of self-publishing – both intentionally and unintentionally. Although often touted as "easy", self-publishing is not for the faint-of-heart. Nonetheless, I've learned to appreciate the hard knocks of this industry. Now I receive joy in sharing my lessons learned with those willing to ride the process of writing and maneuver the journey of evolving one's own book business.

TABLE OF CONTENTS

CHAPTER   SECTION

1   The Self-publishing Hype

2   Primary Publisher Types

3   The $15,000 Mistake

4   The 5 W's & H

5   Calculating Your Costs

6   The Expense Sheet: Do Your Math

7   Writer Versus Book CEO

8   Embrace and Evolve to the Role of Book CEO

THANK YOU

ABOUT THE AUTHOR

CHAPTER # 1
The Self-Publishing Hype

---

*The Truths and Concerns About the
Self-Publishing Business*

In recent years the publishing industry has grown, or rather exploded, exponentially; largely due to self-publishing. Whether writers have been formally schooled or trained at mastering literature and creative writing, the reality that one's experiences and imagination can come out of the mind, be placed onto paper, and go into the world (i.e., hands of a reader), is nothing short of exhilarating.

IS SELF-PUBLISHING EASY?

However, when embracing the self-publishing journey, even the most adroit writer will quickly learn that self-publishing is truly only easy if you're "wired" to run your own book business. Secondly, it's easier when you've laid out the strategy and plan, not only for the project that's in-hand, but the complete evolution of your business. Yes indeed, the only easy part of self-publishing might in fact be the writing — putting pen-to-paper. I attended both high school and college to study journalism, yet never specifically set out to become a published author. I had been interested in writing since first grade. For my first literary work, I labeled myself as an "unintentional" author for my first literary work. Likewise, there was no plan, or even interest for that matter, to self-publish. You see, I had given my manuscript to a publisher, but the production of my book, never took place. The publisher did not acquire the copyright, secure the International Standard Book Number (ISBN), and of course did not print my book. All to my dismay. However, two dear friends (Pastor Richard and Sister Linda Meadows) encouraged me that self-publishing was the way to go. And to my surprise, within weeks I had my book in-hand. I just as quickly learned, that the self-publishing route was not easy, nor was it free, nor could I truly do it all by myself.

With all of the fanfare and promotional energy around self-publishing, those outside the industry (including experienced writers and authors), will learn that it takes time, money, focus, talent, skill and a team to "really" get a book produced. But with so many people celebrating being a published author, it must be relatively easy…right? Well, in my estimation, the easy part is in the writing; the struggle is in the production, marketing, leadership, and evolution of one's book business. And might I add, that whether the literary work is done in paperback, hardback, audio format, eBook or otherwise, book production requires more than a grasp of English literature. Producing a literary work requires industry knowledge. So this literary piece that you're reading right now is my passion to share with aspiring authors "Don't Make This $15,000 Self-Publishing Mistake." If you're already a published author you might be wondering whether there's anything you could possibly learn from reading the

chapters of this book. The answer is a resounding
"Yes!" Even if you have a publishing company
representing you today, there will likely be one or two
nuggets of information that you did not know about
yesterday. So, read on.

WHAT'S THE GREATEST AUTHOR CONCERN?

Depending on which phase of book production you
are approaching or engaged in will likely determine
the issues or concerns that will be present. For
simplicity sake, let's view authoring in three phases:

Phase 1 – Writing the Book – getting the book
information out of the mind and onto the paper. This
includes studying, researching and gathering the
information regardless of the type or genre of
literature that's being prepared.

Phase 2 – Producing the Book – the layout and
formatting of the final book. This includes all of the
steps necessary to get the tangible book product in the
desired visual and even audible formats.

Phase 3 – Selling the Book – the advertising and
marketing of the literary work. This includes the
ongoing creative promotional efforts to place the
literary work in the hands of the targeted audience.
Each of these phases has sub-phases and categories.
There are emotional highs and lows, triumphs and
trials, accolades and regrets the writer will experience
within each phase. However, when I have surveyed

writers, their greatest concerns are about the quality of their work, whether they will be a best-selling author, and how to effectively market their book. A lower-level or non-existent concern is "What's this going to cost me?" As mentioned earlier, the fanfare around the self-publishing industry rarely highlights the expense involved. Yet, this is the one concern that should be addressed sooner rather than later. My best recommendation, is to assess the cost and financials during the "Self-Publishing Strategic Planning Phase." What's that? An essential process often not considered or entertained likely due to an unawareness rather than intentional disregard. This subject will be addressed in the "Writer to CEO" segment of this book.

CHAPTER #2
Primary Publishing Company Types

The Critical Distinctions Between the Seemingly Easy-to-Understand Roles

If there were a prize given to name and define all the types of publishers or publishing companies, there very well might not be any winners. When reviewing the list of publisher types, it might be as short as three or as long as 10 or more. The longer list of types of publishers may include, but not be limited to, Trade Publisher, Mass Market Publisher, Educational Publisher, Scholarly Publisher, Children's Book Publisher, Small Press, Young Adult Book Publisher, Electronic Publisher, Boutique Press Publisher, Hybrid Publisher, Vanity Publisher, and of course, Self-Publisher.

The focus of this book is only three publishing types (Traditional, Hybrid, Self) due to the often broad misunderstanding and/or confusion about these three classifications.

TRADITIONAL PUBLISHING
A traditional book publishing company buys the rights to an author's manuscript. Part of the arrangement includes payment of an advance by the book publisher to the author to secure the book deal. There

are many, but a few of the largest traditional book publishers are HarperCollins, Simon and Schuster, and Penguin Random House.

It's been said that traditional publishers have an attitude of "Don't call us, we'll call you," if they're interested in having you as an author affiliated with their brand. Sounds harsh! I've heard it said that a traditional publisher will not even entertain a self-published author unless he/she can provide his/her book has "legitimately" sold at least 10,000 printed books of the same title. These traditional publisher perspectives may be the very reasons hybrid and self-publishing are in such demand today.

HYBRID PUBLISHING

Hybrid publishing is an emerging area that occupies the middle ground between traditional and self-publishing and therefore includes many different publishing models—basically anything that is not self-publishing or traditional publishing. Hybrid publishing is also referred to as "author-assisted publishing," "independent publishing," "partnership publishing," "co-publishing," and "entrepreneurial publishing." Important to know about hybrid publishing is there is shared cost, shared book production responsibility, shared promotional responsibility, and perhaps even shared ownership of the author's manuscript.

There are easily hundreds, if not thousands, of publishing companies that fall into this category. By Googling "self-publishing companies" you're actually making a search request for hybrid publishers. These companies have teams that will assist the author in getting his/her literary work produced. A few well-known hybrid publishers include, Author House, Xlibris and Outskirts Press. However, there are myriad of publishing companies that will "partner" with the author on the editing, designing, marketing, printing, etc. of the literary work. Partnership and shared responsibility aligns these publishers into the hybrid category. Another tell-tale-sign the author pays for services. Remember, the traditional publisher pays/advances the author due to transference of the ownership rights of the manuscript. Typically an author signing with a traditional publisher will get one-third of the advance on signing, another third upon turning in the completed work, and the last third upon publication.

SELF-PUBLISHING
Self-publishing is the publication of any book, album, or other media by its author without the involvement of an established publisher. In the purest sense, self-publishing occurs when an author handles the entire book publication process, including printing, distribution, and marketing. Author execution of all details during the self-publishing process is also commonly called independent publishing.
Pause a moment to consider whether you, the writer/author, desire to take on full and complete

responsibility to manage "every" aspect of your book process—from writing, to book production, to marketing, to the management and evolution of book project(s). If you are not certain, I encourage you to consider "shopping" your manuscript with Traditional Publishers or partnering with a Hybrid Publisher. On the other hand, if you are definite about self-publishing your literary work, embrace your role as a Book Business CEO and undergo the process of the Self-Publishing/Book Business Strategy Work Session. I know they're out there, but I've yet to meet a self-published author in the purest sense—in other words, one who has taken on 100% of all the publishing responsibilities.

CHAPTER #3
The $15,000.00 Mistake

*The Tough Pill to Swallow and How to Avoid
This Costly Blunder*

When an author ask me to purchase their book, I
typically do. I believe in sowing into the lives and
work of authors. On the other hand, when an author
asks me to read her book, I graciously accept, but give
no guarantee on a completion date—unless I am hired
to provide a formal book review. You see, my favorite
time to read is while traveling...when I have no
distractions. Also, I give no definitive date of
completion because if the book does lure me in, in the
first chapter, it will likely be a slower process of
engaging me in the literary piece. Another reason I do
not give a completion date is because I not only read, I
proofread and edit while reading. I do this intuitively.
I can't help it. Since elementary school I've enjoyed
both reading and writing—two reasons I decided to
study Journalism in high school and college.

A dear friend who's an avid reader mentioned she had
read a book by a local author that she thought was
very good. She added he might be a candidate for the
Authors' Showcase conference and encouraged that he
contact me to learn more. (The Authors' Showcase is a
platform conference/seminar event provided for

authors to formally present their books. The Showcase also provides training and information exchange sessions. My friend is not only an avid reader, she's attended the Authors' Showcase and actively participated during the feedback and discussion segments.)

Within the week that author contacted me and enthusiastically asked how he could participate in the Showcase. I explained it's an annual event, but decisions had not yet been made about the theme, location or date of the next annually conducted Showcase. Nonetheless, the author asked if I would read his book and said he would email me his manuscript because he had no other paperback books on-hand and there was an "issue" with his publisher. I didn't ask any further details because I felt his book would provide not only insight on his writing abilities, but on the management of his literary work. I gave the author no expectation on a date I'd finish his book or provide him feedback.

His manuscript came the same day. I printed it for my travels and during my first evening in my hotel room, I read the first chapter and was hooked! I finished sooner than anticipated—by the end of my 2-week business trip. Yet, as engaging as his memoir was, it required more proofreading and editing. I also wondered whether his memoir would be followed up with a Part-2 book, since every chapter ended as a cliff-hanger.

Unsurprisingly, the author reached out to me for feedback before I could call him. Similar to our first conversation, he was enthusiastic and asked, "So what do you think?" I provided my honest genuine motivating feedback and asked about his publisher and next book. He informed me the manuscript, the one he sent me, was the only version and it was the one that went to print. He added his publishing company had handled the editing and book production, and there was no discussion or consideration about a future book.

I asked how I could be of further assistance and discovered he required help in marketing his book and securing speaking engagements. Essentially, he wanted/needed a Booking Agent. I, like he, was enthusiastic, but advised that he find out from his publisher the marketing services they would offer. Without my probing, he shared he had invested $15,000.00 in getting his book published and received four paperback versions of his book. Marketing collateral? Additional printed book copies? Website? Nope!

But surely he just needed to review his publishing agreement and speak with his publisher to get more details about future publisher services. He stated he had not read his publishing contract, due to the "legalese." Instead, he emailed it to me. In essence, he was requesting I be his copyright attorney.

About a week later the author called again with no news. The publisher stated they had fulfilled their portion of the agreement and he was now left to his own self-publishing competencies and devices...and he wanted my assistance. I invited him to participate in a Book Business Strategy Work Session which would layout all of the components needed to evolve his book to its next phase—which would include the speaking engagements he so eagerly desired and getting the proofreading his book dearly needed. However, the author explained he had invested all he had to give in just one year and his book business coffers were now empty. Yikes! He would now have to truly wear the self-publisher hat and step into the ring as a Book Business CEO...with or without the financial backing to make it happen.

For this first-time published author, the $15,000.00 mistake was not reading his publishing agreement. This was a huge investment, in my opinion, for an initial financial outlay, considering his return. A hard "hybrid publishing" lesson to learn and a tough book-sized pill to swallow. My suggestion, albeit much too late, at minimum was that he hire a copyright attorney to review the agreement. I've since invited him to attend various webinars and conferences, and encouraged him to pursue more about the business of publishing.

By the way, for not reading the "hybrid" publishing agreement of my first book, my mistake was considerably less—$2,500.00. I paid this before I received my product. I should have first read the agreement in full. I should not have paid the full $2,500.00 before hitting clearly-defined milestones in getting my book produced. These milestones would/should have been specified in the contract. Failure to read the publishing contract and making the full publishing payment before receiving the product are big no-no's.

My book also had not been assigned an ISBN or copyright. This, ironically, was good news since it meant I had not assigned my manuscript to the paid publisher. And, glory to God, my path unexpectedly (divinely) intersected with Pastor Richard Meadows and Sister Linda Meadows, a husband-wife team that were familiar with the traditional, hybrid and self-publishing industries. I followed their lead and learned the nooks, crannies, and behind-the-scenes antics of the publishing industry. Now I share what I've learned with others who desire to be published authors or to evolve their book business. But I also caution aspiring and published authors that publishing is an on-going journey where learning and application are essential ingredients to moving through and gaining momentum in the literary business.

Read and get your publishing contract reviewed! Whether an author intends to invest $150.00, $1,500.00, $15,000.00 or $150,000.00 during the first year of publishing, it is sagacious to have a copyright attorney review a contract before signing it.

CHAPTER #4
The 5 W's and H

Questions to Get Answered When Going the Hybrid Publishing Route

In basic journalism and news writing, students learn to answer the questions "Who, What, Where, When, Why, How" for any story covered. The same questions should be answered when the author is selecting a hybrid publisher or publishing partner. Again, unless the author is handling every aspect of his book production on his own, he is likely going to take the route of hybrid publishing for the majority of the book publishing project.

There are many questions that can be asked. However, the author should consider getting the following questions answered **before** signing an agreement with a publishing company. These questions will likely spark further conversation that will surface other questions and answers for the book publishing project:

W   *Who owns the literary work – before, during and after the production of the literary work?*

W   *What is the author's required financial outlay, and what will the author receive for his/her investment?*

W *Where will the author's literary work be publicized?*

W *When will the formal agreement commence and cease?*

W *Why are certain services not provided as part of the contract/agreement?*

H *How will the literary relationship evolve and will there be milestones communicated about the project's progress? How will the parties communicate with one another?*

CHAPTER #5
Calculating Your Costs

*The Key Expenses Authors Will Incur When
Self-Publishing Their Book*

More often than not, when I ask an aspiring author if they have calculated the cost of producing their book, the response is "No." I typically follow this up by asking, "What do you think you should invest for the first year in publishing your book?" The answer typically ranges for $0.00 to $500.00.

Conversely, writers who've researched publishing will respond with a range of $1,000.00 to $3,000.00. For authors who have a life-long ambition of publishing, the response has been, "Whatever it takes." This is a rare response, but common amongst writers who are passionate to get their work in tangible form – sooner rather than later. Below are common book expenses self-publishing authors should anticipate encountering:

BASIC BOOK EXPENSES	OTHER BOOK EXPENSES
• Proof-reading and/or Editing Cost	• Illustration Cost (if applicable)
• Book Cover Design Cost	• Website Design/Maintenance
• Layout/Formatting Cost	• Postage & Shipping Costs
• Print Production	• Payment Transaction Fees
• Marketing Cost	• Formal/Professional Book Review
• Copyright	• Contact List Maintenance
• ISBN	• Administrative Support

CHAPTER #6
Your Expense Sheet: Doing Your Math

Typical Self-Publishing Expenses and Costs

There's a relatively simple and practical way to arrive at a dollar amount that a writer should consider investing in his/her own book project. It's critical in revealing a realistic expense budget that the writer should generate in order to get their book into the hands of readers.

When the self-publishing author completes the Expense Sheet during a Book Business Strategy Session, she is better positioned for the inevitable expense impact. Below is a starter list of book production expenses self-publishing authors encounter. Enter your anticipated first year costs as well as the actual/quoted costs. Disregard any expenses you believe are not applicable:

EXPENSE	ANTICIPATED COST	ACTUAL COST
Proofreading		
Editing		
Book Cover Design		
Illustration		
Layout/Formatting		
Copyright Certification		
ISBN		
Book Production		

[CONT.]

EXPENSE	ANTICIPATED COST	ACTUAL COST
Professional Book Review		
Book Postage & Shipping		
Website Design & Maintenance		
Collateral Design/Production		
Email Distribution		
Legal Advice		
Marketing/Advertising		
Book Launch Event		
Vendor Event(s)		
Administrative Assistant		
Travel		
Literary Training/Workshops/Seminars		
Payment Processing Transaction Fees		
Book Business Advice		
Miscellaneous/Other		
Total		

CHAPTER #7
Writer Versus Book CEO

Understanding the Roles of Writer and Book CEO

Earlier in this book I mentioned that I stumbled into the self-publishing business because I failed to do a very elementary component of the publishing business. I did not read the publishing contract and I paid before receiving my book product. It cost me $2,500.00, yet catapulted me into the publishing business where I was required to not only learn how to get my first book produced in tangible form, but it ironically stretched me into becoming the CEO of my Book Business. Why is this relevant? Well, I also mentioned I had a love for reading and writing. My first grade school teacher planted the seed of journalism which resulted in me becoming a creative writer, winning essay contests and eventually majoring in journalism.

While working as a human resources practitioner, I became editor of my employer's magazine and comfortably would prepare business reports. So I flowed with writing. I had a natural comfort with writing. When I wrote my first book and turned over the completed manuscript to be formatted and produced, I had no understanding of the publishing business. I simply handed over my manuscript and payment to a hybrid publisher and trusted her to finish off the production. [Note: at that time I did not fully understand the role of a publisher, much less know the term "hybrid publisher."] When my book was not produced in time for my planned book launch event, I "stumbled" into the self-publishing arena. Self-publishing, however, stretched me. Thinking beyond writing became my mission. I had to think above the level that only required me to consider receiving a shipment of my books. I had to think like a business owner, a business leader, a business strategist. Strategy is about observing situations through the lenses of finance and accounting, technology, operations, legal, marketing/branding, advertising, staffing, organizational development and logistics. These are the components of a business operation.

Simultaneously, because I'm a self-publisher I had to think and operate tactically (data entry, customer service, clerical, administrative, follow-up/through, surveying, shipping/receiving, cold calling, scheduling, etc.). Understanding the tactical portion is just as significant as the strategic elements because unless you have staff to carry out the tactical responsibilities you're it! And your business might suffer from not getting the day-to-day widget details of your "bookwork" done, which can inevitably impact book sales.

Having the CEO core competencies are an asset in self-publishing. A strategic mindset is essential—innovating, navigating, partnering, collaborating, analyzing, managing ambiguity, motivating, creating, delegating, developing talent, managing change, measuring, transforming, executing flawlessly), are an asset in self-publishing. However, I encourage writers to consider which aspect of book production provides them their motivation and zeal. If the energy only comes from writing, then allow that to be the major lane or stream of flow. On the other hand, if strategy provides just as much satisfaction and excitement, then ride that wave of being some form of a publisher. Better yet, if you have the skill to synchronize writing, strategy, and tactical execution, you likely are wired to be your own Book Business CEO! Most importantly, being the Book Business CEO has a foundational understanding that the book business is a journey which requires on-going learning, application, and execution.

Those who choose to just write will likely find their greatest joy in handing off book production responsibilities to a qualified traditional or hybrid publisher. Those who want to both write and steer their book business can flow in the self-publishing vein, but understand having a plan and team are essential.

The Book Business Journey

CHAPTER #8

Embrace and Evolve to the Role of Book Business CEO

Making the Shift and Enlarging the Territory

"Information is power" is a well-known adage. Yet, the phrase "Applied information is power" has more umph. After all, what good is information if the intended recipient does not walk-it-out? Because, "Education (received) without application is merely entertainment."

If you believe you have a story bottled up inside of you that needs to be told and immortalized by being printed on paper, I entreat you to get started. Embrace the reality that you're an "author" and start your journey. At minimum, get a composition notebook or journal and start jotting your story on paper, or use your audio recording service on your cellphone to start audibly recording your manuscript. Simultaneously, locate an inspiring fellow writer, writing organization, blog site or website and get your energy sparked and reinforced from those common literary passions and interests. Although many writers are said to be loners and fly solo, two (or more) are better than one. You can also glean from the paths others have taken on their journey to becoming published authors.

If you are nearing completion, or now have in-hand a completed manuscript and are trying to determine which publishing route to take, do your research. Gather information on the different types of publishing companies. If you opt for traditional or hybrid publishing, read the contract. If the legalese is too overbearing, secure a copyright or contract attorney to evaluate your agreement, before signing the "deal." Applying the axiom "forewarned is forearmed" is both relevant and wise in the publishing industry.

If you've decided to embrace the role of self-publisher, you have either knowingly or unknowingly stepped into the role of Book Business CEO. Like the writer-author, you now should garner the education and training necessary to get your book produced. If you are not already a business leader, entrepreneur or sole proprietor, embrace the wisdom that tapping into business and leadership information will bolster your development in running your book business. Also, like writing, become linked with like-minded literary experts and enthusiasts. Even if you self-publish only one book, since self-publishing requires a CEO mindset over the course of a book's life cycle, purpose in your heart and mind that you will manage your project with the core competencies of a CEO.

As I mentioned previously, the thrill of getting your words on paper and published for the world to read may drive you (the author) to ignore the significance of thinking like a CEO. The tenacious drive to hold the book in hand and host the book launch party can become so overwhelming that strategic planning and even logical thinking may seem impractical and, perhaps, senseless. More often than I like to hear, authors have admitted that after their book launch has taken place, the thrill was gone. After their warm circle of influence (family members and friends) have purchased the book, the energy to continue, the direction to pursue, the connections to make, the vendor events to attend, the training to invest, all became too tedious and overwhelming. Boxes of books still line the walls of garages. As a result, the thrill of being a published author, award-winning author or even best-selling author wanes or completely evaporates, leaving their book projects abandoned.

My desire is to reignite the disheartened author by developing the business strategy (i.e., information, training and developmental tools and resources) to re-engage and re-connect them with their book business projects. By partnering with these CEOs, they'll now have the support to not only re-imagine, but to revive their book projects with an energy to have their literary work go through a true book business life cycle. These authors will now not only have a plan, but will have the information and CEO skill-building tools as self-publishers to evolve their book business and achieve their desired outcomes.

How does an aspiring self-publishing author differ from a re-engaged published author? Time and experience. The aspiring author has yet to invest the time or resources or experience the ups and downs of publishing. Yet, both the aspiring and published author will learn the essential information of self-publishing and being a Book Business CEO to help them achieve the desired outcomes.

Avoid the $15,000.00 mistake. Read your publishing contracts. Plan and chart the course for your desired book results. Invest appropriately in your book business by beginning with a Book Business Strategy Session. Enjoy the journey!

THANK YOU!

I appreciate that you've taken the time to read my book. I would be further blessed by your candid feedback about this literary work. You may request a Book Business Strategy Work Session and/or send your comments about this literary work to either of the below email addresses:

info@plumblineconsultinghr.com
theauthorsshowcase@gmail.com

You may also purchase my other literary work by notifying me via email or ordering from my Authors' Showcase website at:

www.theauthorsshowcase.com

Kind Regards,

Jill

ABOUT THE AUTHOR

Born in Queens, New York and raised in Staten Island author, media host, entrepreneur and licensed minister Jill-Capri Simms is the youngest of seven children. After receiving her Bachelor's degree in Broadcast Journalism from Syracuse University, she moved to Sacramento, California where she resided with her daughter Capri-Alexis.

Jill and "Alex" relocated from Sacramento to Georgia and then to Central Florida. As an on-going learner, Jill attained her Master's degree in Human Resources Management from Troy State University and later taught HR at the college level.

After more than 25 years working for large national and global organizations, Jill stepped out on faith and launched the human resources consulting firm, Plumb Line Consulting, LLC which primarily focuses on offering specialized HR services to owners of small-/mid-sized companies, non-profit organizations, churches, and ministries.

For pleasure, Jill enjoys hosting the Authors' Showcase writers conference and the Liberating Truth media broadcasts, facilitating workshops, studying the Word of God, writing, reading, traveling as well as discovering the abundant life God desires for His children here on earth.